Cleveland, Ohio Merchants National Bank

Banquet Given in Honor of Truman P. Handy

May 15, 1882

Cleveland, Ohio Merchants National Bank

Banquet Given in Honor of Truman P. Handy
May 15, 1882

ISBN/EAN: 9783744667265

Printed in Europe, USA, Canada, Australia, Japan

Cover: Foto ©Suzi / pixelio.de

More available books at **www.hansebooks.com**

BANQUET

GIVEN IN HONOR OF

Truman P. Handy.

MAY 15TH, 1884,

BY

THE DIRECTORS

OF

The Merchants' National Bank.

CLEVELAND, OHIO:

LEADER PRINTING COMPANY, 116 SUPERIOR STREET.

1884.

TRUMAN P. HANDY, having completed an active service of fifty years in the business of banking in the City of Cleveland, the Directors of the Merchants National Bank, whose President he has been for more than twenty years, desirous of marking an event, of so great public interest, in a suitable manner, as well as of giving expression to their appreciation of the great value of his services as a banker, and also of paying tribute to his character as an eminent citizen, invited the following named gentlemen to be present at a complimentary dinner given him, at the Union Club, May 15th, 1882:

Henry B Payne, Amasa Stone, J. H. Wade, Dan P. Eells, Richard C. Parsons, J. H. Devereux, John W. Allen, Harvey Rice, Rufus, P. Ranney, George Mygatt, Samuel Williamson, Edwin B. Hale, Edwin Cowles, Samuel H. Mather, Charles F. Brush, Sylvester T. Everett, William Edwards, Marcus A. Hanna, John A. Foot, James J. Tracy, and Charles S. Pomeroy, D.D., of Cleveland; C. C. Trowbridge and John S. Newberry, of Detroit; Jenkins Van Schaick, of New York.

The Directors of the Bank were all present: William Bingham, Samuel L. Mather, Selah Chamberlain, George W. Gardner, James Barnett and Edwin R. Perkins.

After the very elegant dinner, served by the Union Club, Mr. Perkins, who presided, arose and said:

Mr. Perkin's Remarks.

We are assembled to-night to pay an affectionate tribute of respect to one whom we have long known and honored. It is now a little more than fifty years since Mr. Handy came to Cleveland, a young man full of promise, of ambition and of hope. He came a stranger among strangers, without fortune and without friends. And to-night amid the varied memories that come to him as, "standing upon the serene heights of age," he glances back through the long vista of the past, I can imagine no greater reason for felicitation than the recol- lection that during all this long period of time, amid all the mutations of fortune, the coming and the going of generations, he has at all times enjoyed the friendship, the confidence, the affection of men like yourselves, the representatives of the business energy, the wealth and culture of Cleveland.

In the life of any one man, fifty years are a very long interval; but they are a very brief space in the life of a nation or of the world. And yet these fifty years have witnessed more great events, more wonderful progress in the arts, in science, in literature, in the development of civil and religious freedom, in mechanical inventions, than any other three centuries in the history of the world. During these fifty years Mr. Handy has witnessed the foundation of a belt of prosperous commonwealths extending from the lakes to the Pacific seas. He has seen this beautiful city growing from a few hundred inhabitants to its present proportions. He has witnessed the expansion of its commerce, the marvellous growth of its manufactures, the development of its railway systems, the founding of its schools and seminaries of learning, the building and endowment of its asylums and hospitals. When he came to Cleveland the snort of the steam horse had never been heard west of the banks of the Hudson. It was twelve years later before Morse was able to give affirmative answer to the interrogatory propounded to Job, and which for more than thirty centuries had stood unchanged: "Canst thou send the lightnings that they may go and say unto thee, Here we are?" It was ten years later still before our distinguished friend (Mr. Wade) had commenced girdling the continent with his system of electric wires and laying the broad foundation alike of his fortune and his fame. It is but yesterday since our young friend (Mr. Brush) has made his name a household word in all parts of his native land, and known and honored in every great commercial metropolis of the world from London to St. Petersburgh; from the Golden Horn to the banks of the Indus, and on the far off Cathay and the Bay of Yokahama. We seem to have realized the dream of the ages. We have discovered the philospher's stone. Intelligent labor transmutes all things into gold.

I may not, my friends, longer detain you from the pleasure of listening to our honored guest. I am sure we can all most heartily unite in the sentiment received by wire, this afternoon, from the eminent historian and statesman, George Bancroft, an early and life-long friend of Mr. Handy:

"Long life and happiness to Truman P. Handy, whom I had the good fortune to introduce to Cleveland; and ever increasing prosperity to the city, of which I was one of the first to discern its unrivalled position."

Mr. Handy, after the applause which greeted Mr. Bancroft's toast had subsided, arose and delivered the following address:

Mr. Handy's Remarks.

My Friends and Mr. Chairman:

I feel a good deal of embarrassment in rising to acknowledge the honor you have shown me by your presence here this evening. It is but once in our lives that a period of half a century in business life can be passed. It is seldom that in any occupation or professional life we are permitted to celebrate fifty years of unbroken service, and more than all, to find one's self surrounded as I do to-night with so large a circle of sincere and confiding friends. I can only thank you all, and especially those who have seen fit to call this pleasant company together on this occasion. I am reminded, as I look around on these pleasant rooms, that I stand within the dwelling that I erected forty-five years ago, and where, with a beloved family, some six years were happily spent under this roof.

It is just fifty years in March last since I came to this goodly city, or rather village of Cleveland, which then boasted of a population of 1,500 inhabitants. My friend John W. Allen was then, and for two years following, the president of the village and one of the prominent and leading men of the place. We are glad he is yet with us, and honor him for that large share of generosity and public spirit that distinguished his early career. The Ohio canal had been completed and opened but little more than a year, and with the exception of three or four leading stores on the hill, the largest share of its business was done on the canal and river. There were no church buildings except Trinity, which stood on the corner of Seneca and St. Clair streets, a plain wooden edifice with a tower.

The First Presbyterian Church had been organized some twelve years previous, but had no house of worship. Its members met in the third loft of Dr. Long's buildings on Superior street, where the American House now stands. In the absence of a minister services were held and a sermon read. During that year Rev. Samuel Hutchings was employed as a preacher. He is still living in New Jersey. We had no public schools. The old Academy on St. Clair street, nearly opposite the Kennard House, was the most prominent place of in

struction. A small wooden building at the foot of the
hill where the new depot now stands was erected the
following year as a Bethel, in which was gathered a
small group of the poorer children and taught by a Miss
Van Tine. The school was supported by private charity,
and here began the public school system of our city.
Some fifty children then attended and were taught without charge. Now the number in attendance in our
public schools is between eighteen and nineteen thousand. We had two hotels, the Mansion House, kept by
Morris Hepburn and afterwards by E. M. Segur, and
the Franklin House, by Philo Scoville, both on Superior
street. There were also two or three smaller ones. The
business of the place hardly extended further on Superior
street than to Bank street, and on either side above that
were dwellings and shops. Peter M. Weddell and Richard Hilliard were the leading merchants. The former
occupied the corner of Bank and Superior streets, both
as his store and residence, where the Weddell House now
stands, and the latter at the head of Superior street, near
the present viaduct. Other prominent merchants were
T. P. May, Irad Kelly, Prentis Dow, Nathan Perry,
McCurdy & Conkling, Joel Scranton and others. Among
the prominent lawyers were Samuel Cowles, S. J. Andrews, Harvey Rice, J. W. Willey, Reuben Wood,
Samuel Starkweather, Leonard Case, and S. Williamson.
My friend H. B. Payne, and the late Judge H. V. Will-
son, came the following year as young law students, and

John A. Foote soon appeared and became a partner of
S. J. Andrews. Among the river men were Charles M.
Giddings, John Blair, N. C. Baldwin and Richard Wins-
low. The principal physicians at the time were Dr.
David Long, Joshua Mills, Dr. McIntosh, and, soon
after, came Dr. E. Cushing, who is still with us. The
only paper then published was the Cleveland Herald,
issued weekly by Seth A. Abbey, the offices being on
Superior street, where the Crittenden store now stands.
A Democratic paper was soon after issued called the
Cleveland Advertiser, afterwards changed to the Plain
Dealer. There were but few manufacturing interests:
a paper mill owned by James Kellogg, a steam flour-
ing mill, at the foot of St. Clair street, by Edmund Clark,
with some smaller establishments. The business of
the place was chiefly in its commerce and as a point
of trans-shipment of the products of the State by the
Ohio Canal. Large purchases were here made of grain
and provisions both for the supply of the Eastern and
Western markets. Chicago came here for her flour and
pork for several years after this period. We had no iron
mills or furnaces for years after this. For all such sup-
plies resort was had to Pittsburgh. No railways were in
existence west of Boston, except the sixteen miles between Schenectady and Albany, opened in the year 1832.
A movement was made by our citizens in 1837 to con-
struct one to Pittsburgh, *via.* Warren, and a committee
sent from here to the former place, of which I was one,

to enlist an interest in that city for its construction, but
the effort failed, and subsequent efforts failed, until some
ten years later, when the Cleveland and Columbus and
the Cleveland and Pittsburgh were commenced.

After glancing thus briefly at the general business of
the place, I must hasten to say that I feel greatly i n
debted to the gentlemen, directors of our bank, and to
many other friends, who have been pleased to refer to
the position I have been permitted to occupy for the past
fifty years as a banker and bank officer in this city.   As
many of you know, I was called here while in the Bank
of Buffalo in February, 1832; was married the following
month, and arrived here on my bridal trip by stage near
the last of March in that year.   The journey was made
in three days from Buffalo, by stage coach, and part of
the way over rough roads.   Hon. George Bancroft, the
historian, in visiting Washington, had found an indebted-
ness of some $10,000 due the United States from the
Commercial Bank of Lake Erie, one of the old chartered
banks of 1816, and that had failed in 1820.   The charter
had some ten years to run.   It was a liberal one, and
Mr. B., coming to Cleveland, was impressed with its
beauty and location, and was sure that it must grow into
a large city.   In connection with his associates, the
Messrs. Dwights, of Boston, Springfield and Geneva,
N. Y., decided to purchase the control of the stock, pay
off the liabilities, and furnish a cash capital adequate to

the wants of the place. This was gradually increased until $500,000 was paid in.

It opened for business on the 2nd day of April, 1832, with Leonard Case as president, and T. P. Handy cashier, the latter on a salary of $1,000 per year. One clerk, Mr. N. R. Haskell, was book-keeper. It was located on the corner of Superior and Bank streets, where the Merchants' National Bank now stands. Its directors, on resuming business, were Leonard Case, Richard Hilliard, Edmund Clark, John W. Allen, Samuel Williamson, John Blair, Peter M. Weddell, T. P. Handy, James Duncan of Massillon, R. Kent of Middlebury, Heman Oviatt of Hudson, David King of Medina, and Alfred Kelly of Columbus, thirteen in all. The bank was successful, and made its dividends of ten per cent. per annum. The village of Cleveland increased in its population and business, and was organized under its city charter in 1836. John W. Willey was its first mayor. It had then a population of nearly 6,000. The following was a year of severe revulsions and a general suspension of specie payments by nearly all the banks of the country in which this bank shared. The Legislature of our State had granted numerous other charters in 1834, and refused to extend the old charters of the State about to expire in 1842. The severe disturbance in business during these years had so crippled these institutions as to force them into liquidation, and this bank, with others, proceeded to wind up its affairs. This was done by the

appointment of three special commissioners consisting of
myself, H. B. Payne and Dudley Baldwin. After some
severe political opposition made to displace us (of which
our friend Mr. Payne can speak), its debt and circulation were paid off, and as no money could in those days
by collected, real estate and city property were taken in
payment of debts without suit as far as possible. This
was in due time transferred to the trustees appointed by
the stockholders, and in 1844 the same was allotted and
distributed to them in payment for their stock. They in
turn appointed me as their agent to sell and dispose of
this large amount of property, some of the most valuable
in the city and now worth many millions; in the mean-
time, while engaged in this service, I had opened a bank
ing office under the name of T. P. Handy & Co., and
continued till the organization of the State Bank of Ohio
in 1845. In November of that year we organized the
Commercial Branch Bank in this city with a capital of
$175,000. William A. Otis, president, and T. P. Handy,
cashier. An excellent board of directors consisting of
W. A. Otis, John M. Woolsey, Jonathan Gillett, N. C.
Winslow and myself were appointed to manage its affairs.
The bank was highly successful and made from 10 to 20
per cent. dividends during the seventeen years of my connection with it, and on winding up its affairs by my suc-
cessors it paid a large surplus to its stockholders. It
was merged into the present Commercial National Bank
so ably presided over by my friend D. P. Eells.

The system of a State Bank and branches, with its circulation perfectly secured, and issued by a "Board of Control" proved the best local system the State had ever enjoyed, and not a dollar was lost to the billholder.

Some trouble was encountered by the passage of onerous and oppressive tax laws, among which was the "Crowbar law." This imposed a tax both on loans and capital, and was resisted by the banks. It was made the duty of the county treasurer, if not paid, to enter the vaults of the banks by force, if necessary, and seize sufficient money to satisfy the claims. Our friend, George C. Dodge, was the county treasurer in 1854, and faithfully performed his official duty. The amount claimed was some $25,800, being nearly 15 per cent. on its capital. This was taken by the treasurer from the vault, the bills having first been marked, and were by him deposited in the vaults of the Cleveland Insurance Company for safe keeping. In the meantime a suit of replevin was commenced in the United States Court at Columbus, and the United States Marshal forcibly entered the vault of the insurance company by night, seized the money, which was identified, and brought the same into court. The law was declared unconstitutional, and the bank settled the claim by the payment of some $3,000. During the past nineteen years this country has enjoyed the benefits of the National bank law, the best banking system ever known. It should be allowed to stand. My experience, as you will see, embraces some

ten years of the old charters of 1816, and two periods of
twenty years each in the State and National systems.
Special charters were granted by the Legislatures of
nearly all the States. In Ohio, free banking was permitted by the act of 1845, on the deposit of the stocks
of this State or of the United States, and the monopoly
of banking has for the past few years been thrown aside,
and is now free to all. The changes both in the mode
of business and its character are very great. We had no
railroads, or telegraphs, telephones, or even express com-
panies in those early days. One of the important duties
of a cashier was to be on the lookout for merchants or
other trustworthy persons going East, by whom a package of bank notes or letters could be sent. The first
package sent off by the bank and entrusted to an honest
merchant, containing only $2,000, was stolen from his
trunk from off the stage while ascending Greenbush hill,
opposite Albany.

The Post Office Department was sustained mostly by
the Northern States, and the rate on a single letter to
New York was 25 cents, and twice that on a double
rate.

Daniel Worley was our efficient postmaster fifty years
ago, and Samuel Starkweather the collector of this port.
Both of these gentlemen were highly esteemed for the
efficient discharge of their duties.

Eastern exchange on New York and Philadelphia at
all times commanded a premium of 1 to 2 per cent., and

during the suspension of specie payments rose from 10 to
20 per cent. premium. Eastern bank notes were as-
sorted and laid aside, and to create exchange, merchants
often purchased flour and provisions to ship to an Eastern market with which to pay for their goods. Under
our excellent National system millions are saved the
people every year. A National bank note issued in
Oregon or Maine is alike par all over these United
States, and for 3 cents our letters may be sent from
Maine to California. The mode of keeping books and
accounts, the copying of letters, the construction of
vaults and locks on the same has greatly improved.
Formerly the larger the key, the more safety was supposed to exist (look at this key in my hand): now no
keys are used, and with time locks and their improved
construction as well as of burglar-proof safes, our treasures defy the most expert lockpicker. We had fewer
embezzlements and bank defaulters in those days than
now, because fewer banks and less of speculation with
other people's money. I congratulate myself, that so far
as I know during all these years there have been no
stealings by bank clerks or directors with whom I have
been associated. I also include in this statement my
associate special commissioners. The old Commercial
Bank of Lake Erie owned the lot occupied by it on the
present site of the Merchants' Bank. It was bought of
Leonard Case and Simon Perkins of Warren for about
$4,000, embracing 100 feet on Superior street and some

ten rods on Bank street, and was occupied both as a
bank and dwelling. In the middle of Bank street stood
an unsightly-looking market house. We had plenty of
dust in summer and mud in winter, but no coal smoke.
In building this dwelling in 1836 I believe I was the first
to introduce grates for burning coal. It was not to any
extent then in use in the city. We were all rich in that
year, at least supposed to be, as far as real estate and
corner lots could make us so, but in 1842 many such
dreams were dispelled. Our merchants were in the
habit of visiting New York twice each year for the purchase of goods, traveling by stage coach and the lake to
Buffalo, and by stage over the mountains to Philadelphia.
They depended for this purpose on the bank for loans
of from $1,000 to $5,000 each at ninety days. The latter was considered a large sum to borrow, and by the
time the goods were received a large part of the time
had expired.

Among the charters granted by the Legislature,
in 1834, was that of the Bank of Cleveland, and organized soon after by the appointment of Norman C. Baldwin, president, and Alexander Seymour, cashier. The
Messrs. Dwights also owned a controlling interest in its
stock. Harman Handy, my brother, became its cashier
in 1838, and soon after died. Its affairs were wound
up by special commissioners, as were other banks of the
State. Until 1845 there were no regular chartered
banks in the city. Their place was was supplied largely

by the issues of Western States, the largest of which
were the notes of the bank of St. Clair, in Michigan,
issued and guaranteed by Jesse Smith & Sons, who afterwards failed. This was called "red dog currency."
Joseph S. Lake issued the notes of the bank of Wooster,
Prentis Dow those of the bank of River Raisin, all of
which in due time failed, and losses ensued to the bill-
holders. The Mormons had a bank at Kirtland, and Joe
Smith pushed out quite a circulation, based on the faith of
"the Saints." It soon exploded, and the church moved
away. This was a period of great disturbance. Bank
notes were classified as "red-dog," "blue-dog," "stump-
tail," Ohio and Eastern. The latter was preferred.
It was not until 1835 and 1836 that many banks existed
in Ohio. The "Miami Exporting Company" of Cincin-
nati, Bank of Chillicothe, Franklin Bank of Columbus,
Urbana Banking Company, Mount Pleasant, Steuben-
ville, New Lisbon, Farmers' Bank of Canton, and the
Western Reserve Bank of Warren, with a few others,
constituted previous to this time the whole list. The
aggregate deposits in the whole State were not equal to
those now in the banks of this city, including the sav-
ings banks. I have thus hastily gone over the business
period of the last fifty years. It has been marked by
great and important changes both in the business and
political world. My friends who are here to night can
better refer to these than I can. It has been an eventful one, both in its changes and progress. In looking

back over the voyage, there have been storms as well as
sunshine, but more sunshine than storm.   I deem it a
matter of devout gratitude to God that I have been permitted to have a part in it, and that my lot has been
cast in so charming a city as Cleveland.   I have been
happily associated most of the time with gentlemen,
directors and bank officers of the highest honor and integrity.   Of this number some twenty have died, and I
myself am reminded by the gathering here of this goodly
company that a half century of business life is but a brief
period; "that our days are as a shadow that passeth
away."

As we draw nearer toward the end I am sure that
these ties of friendship only bind me closer to those I
have so long known but to love and esteem.   Thanking
you all for this hearty reception, and especially the
directors of the Merchants' National Bank for this generous entertainment, I give way to others to whom you
will now, I trust, most gladly listen.

The Chairman:

It was the genial Christopher North, I think, who
said, "The lords of Time's treasury are all on the staff
of wisdom."   I am about to call upon one of them who
came to Cleveland almost sixty years ago, whom none
have ever known but to honor, who enjoys the great
distinction of having been the father of our most excellent common school system, and who has just crowned

a long life of great usefulness by thoroughly organizing
and placing upon an almost self-sustaining basis our
House of Correction—the Hon. Harvey Rice.

Remarks of Hon. Harvey Rice.

Mr. Chairman and Friends:

It is often said that corporations have no souls. I
cannot readily accept this doctrine. It makes too much
of demagoguery. It is evident, say what we will, that corporations lie at the foundations of our commercial prosperity and social advancement. Of these, banks are
among the most important, for the reason that they
furnish facilities which are absolutely indispensible. We
have strong banks in Cleveland, and among them none
worthier of public confidence than the Merchants' National Bank. I believe she is the mother bank of the
city. Her directors and stockholders are well known
as intelligent and reliable men. They all have souls
and human sympathies. Not only that, but the Merchants' National Bank as a corporation has a soul, not
a niggardly one, but a liberal one in the person of her
president. The public know this, and the directors
know it, and appreciate it; and therefore they give this
sumptuous banquet in his honor. Everybody knows
Truman P. Handy, who has been a banker in Cleveland
for the last fifty years. In fact, he was born a banker.
His parents, I doubt not, foresaw at his birth that he

would prove a true man in whatever he undertook, and
hence they named him Truman.

It is indeed a marvel that a banker, in these danger-
ous days, has stood firm amidst seductive temptations
for fifty years, and handled millions upon millions of
money without betraying his trust or being even sus-
pected of misappropriating a single dime. This great
fact in his history is not only a marvel, but a monument
of more value, in a moral sense, than all the millions upon
millions of dollars he has ever counted or discounted.
Few, indeed, are the bankers who have ever earned so
enviable a reputation or set an example so worthy of
imitation. In the course of his career in Cleveland, Mr.
Handy has been officially connected with several differ-
ent banks, some of which, at the time he had charge of
them, were in a sickly and desponding condition; yet
by his skill and tact as a financier he soon restored them
to vigorous health and gave them a standard character.
He has not only lifted banks from the slough of despond,
but has been instrumental in lifting multitudes of poor,
neglected and destitute waifs of humanity from the slough
of moral degradation up to lives of respectability and
useful citizenship. There is heart in what he does. His
benevolence in every good cause has no limit. He has
made money not for the love of it, but for the benevolent uses he could make of it. He bestows silent charities. He has often gone out into the highways and
byways of suffering humanity and relieved their wants

without letting his left hand know what his right hand
did. Yet God knew it was Handy.

The Chairman:

There is near me a gentleman, who has achieved
distinction in many fields of enterprise. He was, while
he remained at the bar, an eminent lawyer; he has had
a large share in building our system of railroads; he had,
according to tradition, quite an experience in banking
at one time; and by a very large part of his countrymen
he has been thought worthy to be a successor of Washington and Lincoln. In this opinion, his old friends
and neighbors, I am sure, all most heartily concur.
"*Omnis Aristippum decuit color, et status, et res.*" I have
the pleasure of introducing the Hon. Henry B. Payne.

Remarks of Hon. Henry B. Payne.

I find it almost impossible to make a suitable speech
upon this occasion, before so respectable and critical an
audience. But I am glad to say a few words, and will
try and recall, to the best of my ability, some facts which
may seem appropriate to this occasion. I came to Cleveland in the year 1833, about fourteen months after Mr.
Handy. It is enough to say that Mr. Handy got the
start of me and has kept it ever since. On my arrival
at Cleveland I entered a law office, and was compelled
to study one year before being admitted to practice in

Ohio. I brought with me to this city one hundred dollars in money—my entire capital—hoping with that, and what I could do in the way of pettifogging, to pick up something in the way of a living, until such time as I should be admitted to the bar. But my capital stock melted slowly away, my business did not rapidly increase, and I soon found myself in straightened circumstances. It became necessary for me to secure a loan of one hundred dollars from the Commercial Bank of Lake Erie. Now, nobody can imagine how difficult it was in those days for a young man to secure a discount at a bank; and I made up my mind, only with fear and for trembling, to apply for the loan. I made out my note $100, drawn up in my best style, and hat in hand, with great trepidation, made my way into the Bank parlor, and found myself in the august and awful presence of the cashier. That cashier evidently was a man of unusual discernment, and had an intuitive perception of the character and value of the young man before him, for he at once said I could have $500 if I wanted it. Under the circumstances, this was a most remarkable declaration, for in those days a man to have credit must be a Presbyterian. Of course, I mean bank credit, and credit at the Commercial Bank of Lake Erie, in particular.

I can certainly say, with truth, that it gives me unusual gratification to be present here this evening, and to take part in paying my tribute of esteem and regard to the character and usefulness of Mr. Handy. I have known that gentleman more than forty-nine years, and I take pleasure in saying, that a truer friend, a more unselfish friend, a better citizen, or more generous hearted, upright man, never lived in this community.

In the days of the bank trouble in Ohio, I was a Democrat, and Mr. Handy was a Whig. It was supposed that I was in sympathy with my party when it refused to extend the existing charters of the banks of the State. But I was not a bank wrecker, and did not believe the Democratic party acted wisely in destroying the banks and wiping them out of existence. It was charged by the party that the banks were fleecing their depositors, and refusing to redeem their paper, with gold or silver, on demand. The action of the Legislature, in refusing to extend the charters, compelled the banks either to redeem their notes in coin, or else go into liquidation; many banks were thus closed. I became an anti-bank attorney, and as such came into close business connection with Mr. Handy. In the very room in which I am now speaking—then the residence of Mr. Handy—I was called into consultation with him and Mr. Henry Dwight, representing the stockholders of the bank, for the purpose of providing a method of closing out the old Commercial Bank of Lake Erie, in such a way as should enable every creditor to receive one hundred cents on the dollar for his claims. At my suggestion, Judge Wood was applied to, to appoint three com-

missioners under the law to take charge of, and wind up
the affairs of the bank; and Mr. Handy, Dudley Baldwin and myself were so appointed. The result of this
action was that the bank paid all its liabilities, and
afterwards divided about sixty per cent. to its stockholders.

Mr. Payne, then, at considerable length, related some
most interesting reminiscences connected with the closing up of the affairs of the bank, and especially gave a
humorous account of the arrest of himself, Mr. Handy,
Mr. Baldwin, the bank commissioners, on the penitentiary charge of embezzling the assets of the bank. Joe
Hayward was the prosecuting witness. It was charged
that the commissioners had sold a parcel of land on St.
Clair street, which had been the property of the bank,
for a wickedly low price. Uncle Leonard Case was
called to testify to the loss, and he swore that the commissioners had received two or three hundred dollars
more than the lot was worth. Other charges came out
in a similar way, but the Court said in dismissing the
prisoners, that they had discharged their duties in an
able, faithful and efficient manner, and regretted that
the Court could not send Joe Hayward before the grand
jury for perjury.

In closing his remarks, Mr. Payne referred to the
excellence of the banking instruction he had received
from Mr. Handy, and said whatever improvement he

had since made was largely owing to the principles of honesty and industry he had learned from him.

The Chairman:

We are glad to have with us to-night a gentleman, who, for almost sixty years has been conspicuous for his eminent ability and distinguished public services. He was the associate of Webster and Clay, and had the great honor of enjoying their friendship and confidence, when they were in the full splendor of their fame. The Hon. John W. Allen, gentlemen.

Remarks of Hon. John W. Allen.

We have not come here to-night to bury our old friend and associate, Mr. Handy, nor to praise him, but to render him that measure of justice which from long observation we think is due him. He has been with us, and of us, for half a century, and if any community should know him thoroughly, this is that one. Fifty years is but a brief space in the history of a nation, or of a large city, but it is about all there is of active, vigorous life in an individual, under the most favorable circumstances, and greatly more than is vouchsafed to most men. We are told by writers, learned in such matters, that but one child in one hundred born into the world lives to the age of sixty-five years, and Mr. Handy has passed that resting place by ten in addition. Within that time all the good properties in a man's nature will

be developed, and the evil ones too will crop out, if any
there be; besides a man's nature is not to be determined
by a single good or bad act as we may think, but by his
ordinary walk and conversation through long years of
exposure and temptations to the wiles of the world. This
much we do know, that no man among us has been more
engaged in helping on the interests of the city in general,
and especially the religious, educational and humane
public institutions, of which we are with good reason so
proud.

He has been doing good and kind acts all his life, not
from a love of popularity or expediency, but from prin-
ciple, and an inherent desire to make men better, happier and wiser—thus making the religion he professes a
practical one for the well-being of all who come within
his influence, and furnishing an example worthy of all
commendation.

This occasion vividly recalls to mind the men who
reorganized the old Commercial Bank of Lake Erie in
1832. There were thirteen directors, including Leonard
Case, Sr., who was made president, and Mr. Handy,
cashier, thus having, you will observe, just a baker's
dozen to manage a small institution, with $100.000 to
work on at the commencement; but it is presumable they
were all good men, for none of them was ever charged
with robbing the bank, so far as I recollect. Mr. Case
was distinguished for his sound common sense, pru-
dence and sterling integrity. Henry Dwight, of Geneva,

N. Y., was the principal capitalist; and, as a man and citizen, of high repute through the whole State. George Bancroft was the principal negotiator in the purchase of the charter. He was not then known to fame, but lives to earn and enjoy a world-wide reputation of enviable character.

Half a century has passed—a generation and a half has since been born, lived and died, and in good degree forgotten; the grass grows over the graves of all the immediate actors in the principal scenes referred to, excepting only the venerable George Bancroft, Mr. Handy and myself, and it will not be long before the death list will be completed. Generations come and go like the billows of the ocean, and like them disappear and are forgotten; and so it will be with us; and still the great globe will roll on and on, its inhabitants, forgetful of the past, in happy enjoyment of the present and bright anticipations of the future, will travel on till they reach that goal from which there is no return, and join that great procession that knows no ending.

The Chairman:

I am reminded that there is a gentleman before me, who in early life was a learner in Mr. Handy's business school. His subsequent career has been a great honor alike to himself and his early instructor. He has achieved distinguished success in other lines of business, as well as in banking, so that now he is almost as well known as a railroad man among bankers as he is a

banker among railroad men.   I take pleasure in calling
upon Mr. Dan P. Eells.

Remarks of Mr. Eells.

Mr. President and Gentlemen:

We have assembled this evening to do honor to a
man whose name has been a household word in Cleveland for half a century.   It is not a common thing that
a man lives in the same community for so long a time;
and yet, when you think of it, the mere fact of having
lived even for fifty years, and in the same community,
is not a matter of great importance.   The biography of
the oldest man that ever lived is summed up in a very
few words: "And Methuselah lived a hundred and
eighty and seven years, and begat Lamech.   And Methuselah lived, after he begat Lamech, seven hundred, eighty
and two years and begat sons and daughters.   And all
the days of Methuselah were nine hundred, sixty and
nine years, and he died."   It has been said that the
epitaphs of most men, who live even to the end of the
alloted time, if properly written, would read: "Born on
such a day, and died on such an other, with an interval
of three score years and ten."   But to have so lived in
a community as to give tone and direction to its thought
and life; to have so impressed his own life upon the
public life, that every important movement in society
takes the direction that he gives it, so that the history of

the city where he lives cannot be written without the mention of his name; to have become identified with every public charity; to have been known for fifty years as a public benefactor—a friend of the poor, a helper of the helpless; I say, to have lived in a community with such a record as his, greatly entitles a man to the respect and honor of society. I think I do not exaggerate when I claim for Mr. Handy some such record as this.

I have as boy and man known him for forty years. During the greater part of that time I have been immediately associated with him, both in business and social life, and I am sure that no man I have ever known has approached nearer to my ideal of true manhood than he. Never a very wealthy man, as that term is generally understood—his benefactions have blessed the entire city ever since he came to live in it. Never a politician —his vote and his influence have been potent in securing good government and a healthy administration of the law. Never a great scholar—he has given generously of his time and money to encourage, maintain and elevate the standard of education. Never an extremist in temperance, or a bigot in religion—his voice has always been heard in defence of sobriety and good order, and in denunciation of every form of intemperance; while as a Christian, he has been a "living epistle, known and read of all men."

But I must not take up your time. I see before me, men who have stood shoulder to shoulder with Mr.

Handy, during the entire term of his life in Cleveland;
men, whose four score years and more, entitle them to
be heard on such an occasion as this. As we think of
such men, who look back upon a long life well spent,
and forward to a few more years, and then a peaceful
entrance into a life of happiness onward, how attractive
does a useful, trustworthy life become? A career of pleasure, the greed of wealth, a selfish, sordid, worldly life—
those fascinating, but illusory visions, which glow before
our youthful eyes in life's young morning, how they fade
and wither, when advancing years afford us a juster,
worthier conception of the great end and objects of our
being! "We live in deeds, not in years; in thoughts,
not words alone. We must count time by heart-throbs,
not by figures on a dial. And he lives most, who thinks
most, feels the noblest, acts the best!"

The Chairman:

I think I will now call upon a gentleman, whose
eminent career at the Bar and upon the Bench, consti-
tutes the most splendid tribute to the superiority of the
commonwealth over the empire. Judge Ranney, gentlemen.

Remarks of Judge R. P. Ranney.

Judge R. P. Ranney said he was neither a capitalist
nor a banker, nor in any way related to them. He
had known Mr. Handy for many years, and if asked to

decribe him to one who had never known him, would prefer that Mr. Handy should not be present, for he would say some very flattering things of him. But with the gentlemen who were present, it did not become an impecunious young man with a sore throat to say much. He was afraid if he did, that the result might be similar to what it was in one of the early cases in which he was an attorney for the defense. The opposing counsel had made a strong argument to the jury. Judge Ranney had only time to state the points in his case before the court adjourned for dinner, but after noon he spoke two hours. Judge Ranney said he was very much afraid of his case. The jury was out a long time, but finally came in with a verdict for Ranney's client. He afterwards asked 'Squire Barnett, who was on the jury, why they had been out so long. The Squire said: "When you stopped at noon, the jury was on your side; but when you went on for two hours, in the afternoon, you split 'em up even, and came pretty near beating your suit." The Judge said he feared that if he talked long about Mr. Handy he might throw some suspicion on his character.

The Chairman:

We have with us a distinguished gentleman from our sister State of Michigan, eminent in every station he has filled, at the Bar, in the management of great business interests, and in public life—the Hon. John S. Newberry, of Detroit.

Remarks of Hon. John S. Newberry.

Gentlemen:

It is with no ordinary feeling of pleasure that I accepted your kind and courteous invitation to this hospitable board this evening, where you have assembled to do honor to one whom I have learned to love and honor in former years.

Some twenty odd years ago, one summer day, I walked up and down before his bank, with fear and trembling, because I was seeking his presence to ask him for the most precious gift he had in his power to bestow—the hand of his only daughter. But nerving myself, I entered, and blushingly preferred my request; receiving no answer, I looked up and found him more agitated and disturbed, and I really believe more frightened than I was. Of course his banker's instincts prevailed; I was to be trusted until he could write to his correspondent, another banker in Detroit; one whom Michigan has been always glad to honor, and who has been so honored for more than fifty years, and who is here your welcome guest, to-night, the Hon. C. C. Trowbridge, of Detroit. The answer he gave was probably satisfactory, and so it happens I can join with you to-night in rendering honor to Truman P. Handy for all personal and public considerations, which have been so ably and entertainingly brought to your notice by the friends who have addressed you. But I owe him for more than any of you can think, or even dream. I owe him for more than a score of years of perfect domestic happiness, and a home without a cloud or shadow.

No reader of history, gentlemen, can fail to be impressed with the fact that the character of a Nation, of a State, a city, or community, is indelibly impressed by its founders, its early settlers; and such characters are after reproduced in the general character of such Nation, or city, in after years. Cleveland was extremely fortunate in that respect. And the impress given by Mr. Handy, and many others I could enumerate of fifty years ago, some of whom are now present, is seen in the grand, benevolent, educational, charitable and religious institutions, that grace your beautiful city to-day.

Men take too little heed of such early influences; but they are potent for good or evil for years,—probably for centuries. A notable instance of two places in Michigan, but a few miles apart, within my own knowledge: The two villages were settled about the same time. One by a God-fearing, honest, industrious colony from New England, and kindred spirits, ready for all good words and works. The other, by men who came simply to make money and look out for self.

In twenty-five years, one was a beautiful, prosperous, well built village, with fine churches and homes; well appointed schools, with an intelligent and religious community. The other was a scrawny, unfinished, dilapidated town; with unfinished churches and decrepit school houses; but with two well furnished distilleries in active operation.

From the young men of the first village went forth into active life—ministers, professors of colleges, noted men of high rank in our army, men standing high in scientific institutions, a Governor of Virginia, judges, members of Congress,—men high in honor in our own State. From the other, I only recall one man of any note; and he only became somebody, after passing middle age as a nobody in that town, and leaving it.

It is thus that characters are stamped on nations and communities. Cleveland may well be proud of its early founders.

For nearly a quarter of a century, gentlemen, I have known and loved him whom you honor to-night. I have seen him under almost all circumstances: when as a man and a citizen he has walked among you and gone out and in before you. To me, he is and always has been, and will be, the ideal of what a Christian business gentleman should be.

All business, charitable, benevolent matter—carefully, earnestly, faithfully, conscientiously and promptly attended to, as if they were a religious duty; and to him they were and are. There is no class of men that stand higher in the esteem and respect of their fellow citizens than bankers—no class to whom more confidence is given. And one who has stood among you in active banking business for twenty, thirty, aye, fifty years, with unsullied name, needs no words of mine to speak his praise; nor can words add to the luster of his character.

Think of it, men! Fifty years in active life as a banker! Fifty years in the strong, daily light of the public view; through whose hands the wealth of a city, the credit of its merchants, and its professional men—its whole mercantile life—has passed, year after year, and not one act, not even a shadow, to dim the luster of the life and character thus exposed to view.

Look again! For fifty years the history of the church, to which he belonged, of this city, and of this State, could not be written, if you write not the name of Truman P. Handy on almost every page.

To whom do the benevolent and charitable enterprises turn for cordial support, active sympathy, and the helping hand, quicker, and with more surety of aid, co-operation and hard work, than to him.

And who shall speak for the hundreds and thousands of the worn and weary; of the poor and lonely; for the sick, unfortunate and unknown, who have been cheered, helped, strengthened and given courage by him. You and I will never know, until the secret of all hearts are revealed before the great white Throne.

But time fails me; words fail me. You, my friends, have known him better and longer than I; but in all places in this great land, aye, in the whole world, it is and always will be, that it is among those who believe in, and who strive to act up to, the strong, earnest, deep-seated principles of God's truth, that we look for the doers of good—the leaders in all good works: the men to whom all turn instinctively, when humanity suffers and needs relief, when evil is rampant and needs to be attacked and put down; when sorrow and suffering prevails and man needs consolation and kindly ministry. In all such cases, an appeal to the man, you honor tonight, met with a hearty, quick response.

I know you have many men, in this city, of this class, some of whom I see before me: but would to God every city in the land had ten thousand such; if it were so, the millennium would not be far off.

Such are the men, no matter what treasures they may still have on earth, yet their greatest treasures are laid up in Heaven where they are registered; and "their works do follow them."

The Chairman:

We will now hear from one of Mr. Handy's distinguished railway friends—Gen. J. H. Devereux.

Remarks of Gen. J. H. Devereux.

Mr. Chairman and Gentlemen:

Deeply appreciative of the honor and pleasure which attends a participation in this remarkable anniversary occasion, I respond to your call.

And, suggested by what has been so well said by the friends who have spoken,—with this one thought uppermost in mind,—the potency of individual character in a people's advancement.

Centuries ago, under the bright sunlight of an oriental sky, certain men were admiring the massive walls and sculptured marbles of one of the greatest temples of the world. And with pointed finger of admiration they exclaimed to the Master, who walked with them: "What manner of stones and what buildings are here!" The Master's reply must have sounded wondrously: "There shall not be left one stone upon another that shall not be thrown down."

But, whilst that grand building was to crumble in the dust, and the site of its very foundations forgotten, the act of one of the humblest persons within its walls that day has been perpetuated in the world's history forever. It was that act of beneficence of the poor Widow,—the gift of all that was hers for the good of others.

So material progress counts less in the world's advancement than the righteousness,—the right-doing, the right-acting,—which exalteth a nation.

The true greatness of the State lies in the right-mindedness of its people,—in the character of its citizens. Such as those whose names are honored by all of us—whose acts and deeds shall speak of, and for them, in the growing expanse of this broad land for long years to come; whose work in ennobling and elevating humanity shall outlast the iron and the marble, and with the results of such life and labor, blessing, and blessed in the doing of good to man, and upholding the integrity of the Commonwealth.

And with these stands he whom we honor to-night. He, who for half a century, has been patient in right-doing: who, steadily urging forward the material development of city and land, has ever been regardful of the needs of the true weal of people and State.

Egypt, with her grandeur; Greece, with her literature; Rome, with her prowess:—all have been, and are not. But the great Republic, whose citizens are these of whose representative is Truman P. Handy, shall flourish and abide forever.

The Chairman:

At my right is the oldest banker present. Born in the closing year of the last century, he has lived to witness all the wonderful progress of the present. Though an octogenarian he still retains all the freshness and elasticity of youth; so much so that it would appear that he must have found the fountain of perpetual youth, for the discovery of which the Spanish knights so persistently labored in vain. In his life, as a pioneer banker he persistently fought the " wild-cat," " red-dog," and various other untamed financial beasts of his time, and came out of the contest without a scratch. The Hon. C. C. Trowbridge, of Detroit.

Remarks of Hon. C. C. Trowbridge.

The Chairman:

My first duty is to thank you and the Directors of the Merchants' National Bank, for the invitation to join you and them in rendering honor to the gentleman who sits by my side,—my tried friend of fifty years,—with whom I have often taken sweet counsel: and, also, on occasions which tried the souls and mettle of men— councils of great gravity. I come not to praise my friend. The effulgence of a pure life of half a century, permeating the social and business circle in which he lived and moved, and throughout the State of his adoption, and this goodly gathering of old friends, and true, are far more eloquent than any words of mine could be.

Mr. Handy has requested me to give some reminiscences of our past life as bankers. You have just passed around this festive board, and handled, the iron key which my friend used to carry in his vest pocket, and which in its day has been the faithful guardian of millions of money. As I lift it up, in weight some pounds, and in length a foot, I am carried back to the time, nearly sixty years ago, when, as a young banker, I was elected to the custody of a similiar, but larger one. Mine had the advantage of a lock within itself, in the form of a bolt inserted in the end and secured by a secret spring. We frequently gave it to loungers as a puzzle. Our vault door corresponded in simplicity,

being formed of bars of iron, bolted to cross bars, and
open enough to admit air into the vault.

I have no accurate knowledge of the history of banking in Ohio. Judge Burnet in his valuable *Historical
Notes*, states that when the Northwest Territory was set
off, under Dane's ordinance of 1787, they had no bank
of issue, and that they anticipated the receipt of revenue
by orders upon the territorial treasury, and that when
the circulation became redundant these fell below par.
When I went to Michigan, in 1819, there were many
amusing stories told about the currency which had been
improvised during the then recent wars with England, in
order to aid the Commissaries and Quartermasters on
the frontier. Among the new banks there was one
called "The Owl Creek Bank." The vignette on its
notes was a likeness of the bird of wisdom, and when
the notes began to lose credit, a genial French inn-
keeper at the River Raisin announced that he did not
receive the bills "dat go whoo! whoo!"

As to Michigan territory, organized in 1805, Governor
Hull and the three territorial judges, who constituted
the legislature, with power to "adopt from any of the
original States, such laws as were suited to the necessi-
ties of the territory," granted to some Boston fur traders,
late in 1806, a charter for the "Bank of Detroit." The
grantees erected an edifice of brick, one story high,
thirty feet square—divided into bank parlor, vault and
banking office. They issued notes, specimens of which

are preserved by the Historical Society; but early in
1809, Congress revoked the charter, probably because
the "suitableness and necessity" did not appear. The
same premises were occupied by the Bank of Michigan,
organized in 1818. Even then, there could not have
been much necessity for a bank, inasmuch as two years
later, when, as Deputy Marshal of the United States, it
was my duty to make a fair copy of the census, the total
population between the Canada boundary line and the
Mississippi, and north to the Red river, was less than
nine thousand. However, twenty thousand dollars was
paid in, and the bank continued in operation until
1824, when the stock was purchased by the Messrs.
Dwight, and Mr. Benjamin Day came on from Mas-
sachusetts to take charge, but not liking the place he
declined, and Mr. G. P. Hastings was sent from the
Bank of Geneva, in February, 1825, to succeed him.
Mr. Hastings soon discovered signs of a defalcation, but
so great was the confidence of the directors in the cashier, that Mr. H. was in danger of being declared the
culprit, until he showed the directors that in spite of
written weekly reports and repeated countings, the
the cashier had not, in the seven years of his service,
opened a personal account with himself, and yet his
teller's statement balanced to a cent every day; and that
fifteen thousand dollars, three-fourths of the capital, had
gone "where the woodbine twineth." The board gave
Mr. Hastings *carte blanche*, and the result was a tussle

over the big key, Hastings being the victor and myself
being appointed its keeper.

Messrs. Edmund Dwight, of Boston, Jonathan Dwight,
of Springfield, Henry Dwight, of Geneva, and the sons
of Jonathan, were men of high honor, great sagacity and
large wealth. Their investments in western banks, at
Buffalo, Cleveland, Massillon, Monroe and Detroit
amounted to millions. They never borrowed a dollar
from these banks, and when the time of trial came, after
the suspension of 1837, they endeavored to preserve
their escutcheon free from the taint of failure by advancing large sums, (to the Bank of Michigan three
hundred thousand dollars); and yet these gentlemen
were stigmatized by the anti-bank people as robbers. I
feel that this avowal is due to their memory.

All went well with the Bank of Michigan until the
apple of temptation came in the form of the deposits of
the public moneys. The local banks were flattered with
their appointment, and were urged by the Secretary of
the Treasury to show their ability to perform the office
of a United States Bank, by lending the public money
and making it plenty among the people. Very soon
there arose a spirit of speculation which turned the heads
of bankers, and statesmen, and capitalists, and in two
years the most sagacious men found themselves inextri-
cably involved in profitless enterprises. The South Sea
scheme had found a parallel in the craze, and the result
was equally disastrous with the fall of that bubble. An

old French gentleman said to me one day in 1839, that
it reminded him of a boy blowing up a bladder and
another boy sticking a pin into it. Late in 1836 the
United States Treasurer began to issue his drafts upon
the deposit banks in sums of one hundred thousand to
five hundred thousand dollars, and by the first of May,
1837, the two deposit banks at Detroit, which had held
more than three millions of public money, were drained
very low. They thought they must close their doors.
I had resigned my cashiership a year before the 10th of
May, and only knew of the struggle as a spectator; but
on that day my old directors sent for me and informed
me that they must close their doors. I looked into their
affairs and said to them, "Don't do that. General suspicion is imminent. Hold on pluckily, and in a few days
you will be relieved. I will prepare a card for you, so
that if you must close, the people will know why." They
approved the suggestion, and this card I have as a
souvenir. Pardon this piece of egotism. Without it I
could not tell you how narrowly the Western banks
escaped the accusation of having caused the great catas-
trophe.

On the 15th of May there came to my house, early in
the morning, a gentlemen who owned an interior bank
a hundred miles west of Detroit. He had ridden express from New York with the news of suspension in
that city on the 10th of May, stopping at Albany, Utica
and Buffalo, to attend impromptu meetings of the citizens,

who with one accord resolved that their banks must suspend "in self defense." He exhibited the handbills of proceedings, procured a meeting of our citizens in the city hall, the United States Judge presiding, and at noon he mounted a fleet horse, and in twenty-four hours was at his own bank.

Thenceforward, through sleepless nights and days of worry, bankers led their lives, for several years, before the country survived. Suspension did indeed create a sigh of relief; but unhappily the debtor class construed the relief acts as made for them as well as for the banks, and they relaxed their efforts. Money grew scarce: lands were unsaleable; a large infusion of bankrupts got into the legislature; two-thirds acts were passed, and men actually purchased Government lands at a dollar and a quarter per acre and turned them over to the sheriff at two-thirds of ten dollars. Among other modes of relief, our legislature passed an act to regulate free banking. A certain class, like the Adullamites of old, rushed into free banking, and in a few months two millions of dollars, presumably secured by lands, were thrown upon the community. In a few months more our Supreme Court declared the act unconstitutional and every contract under it void. No words can convey to you, gentlemen, a true idea of the state of things in the West from 1835 to 1845. *Mais nous avons change tout cela.* Through much tribulation, we have come to possess and enjoy a banking system superior to any the world has known, under which the people have attained a degree of unexampled prosperity.

Mr. Chairman, I am ashamed of myself for having taken up so much of your time. You will, I hope, pardon the garrulity common to great age. My friend Handy and myself spent a summer together at the seaside a few years ago; and we used to repeat these same stories to each other every day. "Panting time toils after him in vain." Long may he live to enjoy the memories of this day.

The Chairman:

I will now call upon our distinguished friend to whom we are always glad to listen, and who never needs an introduction to a Cleveland audience—The Hon. R. C. Parsons.

Remarks of Hon. R. C. Parsons

Mr. President:

At this late hour, I am admonished that "silence is golden," and I fear, in the brief moments I shall occupy your time, I may not be able to say anything of special interest to you, or give satisfaction to myself,—for this is an extraordinary occasion, and demands more than passing notice. Here are the pioneers of old Cleveland; and here are the active, representative men, of all professions, of new Cleveland. At the head of the table

are some of the antedeluvians—or, at all events, men
older than the State in which we dwell; men who can
tell how Ohio looked on that bright morning, when in
all the freshness of her virgin beauty, she came a blush-
ing bride, bringing her ample dowry into the Union.
I have listened with great interest to the revelations
made by these gentlemen,—the confessions they have
seen fit to give us. We have learned what bright and
promising men they were in early life, and how sharp
they grew as they became older and wiser. All the
secrets of their banking life are before us, and we have
learned how easy it was to give the country a sound,
reliable, specie-paying currency, without the aid of any
specie at all,—how they transported their promises to
pay to distant portions of our happy land, in the vain
hope, that the travelers would never return; and when
they did come back, and importunate creditors pressed
their bills for redemption, they locked the great doors
of the bank vaults with their ponderous keys, and pro-
curing certificates of good character from all the lawyers
and respectable citizens of the town, declined to redeem
on the ground that it would embarrass a public and much
needed institution, if not destroy its usefulness, by bringing it to a premature end altogether. All this, and much
more of the early life of these gentlemen, we have listened
to with profound interest. And in view of their trials
and successes, we give them our hearty sympathy and
respect.

I first met Mr. Handy about thirty-five years ago.
He was a remarkably comely man at that time—though
nobody would suspect it now—with a wealth of dark
hair, a clear, boyish complexion, and a smile like a benediction. He gave me a warm welcome to Cleveland, a
friendly grasp of the hand that made one feel at home,
and with pleasant words asked me to come to him if in
any way he could serve me.

A single anecdote will illustrate his character better
than any eulogy. During the war in 1862, I was appointed Collector of Internal Revenue at Cleveland. It
was necessary that I should give bail for a large amount
to secure the Government against loss. Knowing that
it was then the custom for Country Treasurers to pro-
cure bail from the monied institutions in which they
deposited their collections, and that it was regarded a
mere matter of business, I called upon my friend, Mr.
Amasa Stone, who was then a director of one of our
banks, (the Second National), and suggested that he and
his co-directors, sign my bail-bond, and his bank should
receive the deposits. He promptly agreed, so far as he
was concerned, and said he would lay the proposal
before the board. He did so, but the board declined,
on the ground that in giving bond for my own conduct,
they became responsible for my deputies in other coun-
ties. I never had any respect for the opinion of that
board of directors from that day to this one. Not
wishing to ask my personal friends to sign the bond, I

was about to decline the office, when Mr. Handy, meeting my father-in-law, Judge Starkweather, asked him
when Mr. Parsons was to begin his work, and if his
bond had been given. The Judge explained the situa-
tion, said that Mr. P. was about ready to decline the
place, as he did not wish to put himself under personal
obligations to any one, by asking for bail. Mr. Handy
at once said, "I know Mr. P. and can trust him fully.
Send his bond to me." This was done, and when it was
returned it had upon it security to the amount of a million of dollars! The Secretary of the Treasury wrote
me the bond was equal to any filed in the State. That
is the sort of a man Mr. Handy is. I am glad to say
he suffered no loss. When my accounts amounting to
over $12,000,000 were settled, a balance was found due
me of seventy-five cents, a draft for which, signed by
the financial officers of the Government, was duly sent
me. I had it framed, and it now hangs in my library, a
memorial of the wealth and opulence one may reach by
being an officer of the United States.

We have heard to-night much about old Cleveland.
Let us have something of the new,—that Cleveland
famed far and wide for her beauty, just now arraying
herself in her garments of green. Around me are the
men who have made our city and the age famous—men
who built the railroads—covered the land with the wires
of the telegraph—founded the great iron mills—invented
the electric light, and erected temples of charity for the

use of suffering humanity. There sits a gentleman, (Mr.
Wade), whose generosity is only equaled by his modesty.
On yonder street rises a costly edifice of stone, a model
institution, ample for all its needs, a home built for the
little homeless children, the orphans of the city. There
they are reared under kindly influences, with Christian
watchfulness, trained for lives of usefulness and honor.
That is only one of the gifts of that gentleman to Cleveland.

Here sits a citizen, (Amasa Stone), who by close
attention to business and frugal habits, has amassed a
sufficient competency to keep him from the danger of
absolute want. He was found strong enough to lift
from its foundations, where it had been imbedded among
the mosses for half a century, the Western Reserve College, at Hudson, and deposit it in Cleveland, endow it
with an ample fortune, where I trust it will long remain,
"a cloud by day and a pillar of fire by night," to lead
the youth of our land to ways of education and honorable ambition. On my right sits a gentleman whose
name has become a household word in the world of
science, (Mr. Charles F. Brush). A few years ago he
was a simple lad, a country boy of Cuyahoga County,
the son of a farmer. Fitting himself for college and
graduating with honor, he became an inventor, and is
known as the father of the electric light. We are proud
that it is to Americans the world owes the debt of
making the lightning do the bidding of man. It was

an American, Doctor Franklin, who caught the electric
messengers from the angry clouds. It was Morse, an
American, who harnessed them for use. It was Field
and Wade who made them cross oceans and span con-
tinents in the daily service of the world; but it was
reserved for Brush—the farmer's son of Cuyahoga—to
seize the reins lying upon the backs of the fiery coursers,
and like another Aurora guiding the chariot of the sun
through the portals of day, to mount his triumphal car
of silver, and driving into the darkness of the night,
leave behind him a train of phosphorescent splendor,
which glows, and glitters, and sparkles, illuminating the
earth from pole to pole.

And at this gathering let us remember that new Cleveland holds the sacred ashes of her son, that distinguished
scholar, soldier, statesman, patriot and chief magistrate,
General Garfield. Though his virtues and his fame
require no monument to perpetuate their memory, yet
soon there will arise over his remains one of the most
magnificent monuments known to modern history—the
gift of his appreciative and admiring countrymen. We
owe a debt to Mr. Payne and Mr. Wade for their in-
valuable services in pushing forward this great work.
Let me beg of them, that when the noble memorial shall
be completed, where it will stand forever, and become
the Mecca to which thousands of pilgrims will annually
resort to learn new lessons of faithfulness and patriotism,
they will place upon the shady side of the monument,

by the cypress and the willows, those piteous words of
the dying President, "*Strangulatus pro Republica*," and
upon the other side, where bronzed dome, and tower,
and minaret, shall glow and smile to meet the morning's
sun, those other words dear to every patriotic heart:
"*Dulce et decorum est pro patria mori.*"

I close with only a word for Mr. Handy. During all
the years of my manhood, he has been to me a faithful,
devoted, unselfish adviser and counselor. I may say
with truth he has been to me a guide, philosopher, and
friend. For him I entertain the sincerest gratitude,
affection and respect. I trust his future years may be
many, and as honorable to himself as the years that are
past. Of him I can say, as was most happily said of
another,

> "So if I ever win the home in Heaven,
> For whose sweet rest I humbly hope and pray,
> In the great company of the forgiven,
> I shall be sure to find old Daniel Gray."

The Chairman:

Near me is the gentleman whose whole life has been
redolent of good deeds and gentle charities, the Hon.
John A. Foot.

Remarks of Hon. John A. Foot.

Mr. Chairman:

Though I have been a resident of Cleveland, as
long as Mr. Handy, less one year, still I cannot remem-

ber that any *public notice* has ever been taken *of this fact.*
Certain I am, that the *élite* of the city have never made
such a grand reception for me as they are this night
giving our friend. And Bancroft has never denied that
he had a hand in getting me here, as his communica-
tion, to-night, tells us that he had in giving to us Mr.
Handy. Now, while I will not conceal *my surprise* at
this, I am not here to complain of it, but will merely
remark, in passing, that it is, indeed, a real honor to be
thus distinguished by such a banquet, and such a
presence as now confronts me.

But though not thus distinguished, I have been near
enough to Mr. Handy all these years to be able to testify
that he richly deserves all these honors: that his has
been the highest character; the most tried integrity; the
simple, honest, hard work in the various positions he
has been called upon to fill; while all these traits have
been grandly equa'ed by his rare good sense and
princely benefience.

To most men it is enough to be distinguished in *one*
department. Indeed, so impressed with the truth of
this thought, are we, that we have come to say: Be-
ware of the man of one idea! Mark and see the power
of the man who makes a *specialty* of any thing. How is it
with Mr. Handy? He is, and has been, *The Banker,*
The Financier,—head and shoulders above all others in
the vicinage.

You want to start a railroad; you tie to Mr. Handy as the first man and when you come to the practical work you find you have made no mistake. He is equally useful here as in the bank. Nay, and the same can be said of him in all the rounds of business.

But we come to another field: We want to look at the moral and religious—the educational and the benevolent work of the community. Here we have turned, and do still turn to Mr. Handy, as instinctively as in business matters. He plans for us; he gives. He is the Sabbath School superintendent,—as distinguished as the bank president, and a mainstay in our countless benevolences as well.

I deem this recognition of Mr. Handy a most happy thought. It is not only due to him, but it is due *from* the community in which he has lived and labored. It is due to this and other communities, that such a life should be held up as an example. It honors each of us, and all of us, who are participating in it.

The Chairman:

There are many others to whom we should like to listen; but I am admonished that we are approaching the small hours, when all sober minded young people should be asleep, and so I will only call upon one more gentleman. He has for a number of years sustained very close relations to Mr. Handy. The Rev. Dr. Pomeroy, his pastor.

Remarks of Rev. C. S. Pomeroy, D.D.

Mr. Chairman and Gentlemen:

I suppose I am summoned last, with a view of giving you a sort of pastoral benediction.

Pardon a word of eulogium upon yourselves, as you call me at the close of this delightful reunion. It has amazed me to listen to your wise and brilliant talk this evening, when I know by theory and present experience, that no time is less auspicious for happy speech, than when a man's nervous energy is centering itself upon his digestion.

But one might as well say "don't boil" to a kettle over the fire, as don't become joyful, congratulatory, enthusiastic, on so rare an occasion as this. Many men can never bear prosperity, and a still larger number cannot bear the prosperity of others, but it appears that you can do both.

In such a banking atmosphere, the influence is contagious. It draws large drafts upon one's sympathies. It induces a monstrous deposit of good wishes, and precludes the necessity of making any check upon enthusiasm, or discounting a single one of the happy collateral influences of the hour.

Still, these old associates should be the spokesmen to night; those who have summered and wintered with our honored guest, rather than any newer friends of later date. It is a joy for me, however, to drop my tribute with the rest.

You, sir, have spoken of me as his pastor. For the nine years that I have been privileged to know Mr. Handy, I have never been quite certain whether I was his pastor, or he mine—so constantly have I been instructed and enriched by his association and example. At the outset I entertained a high opinion of our friend, but growing as it has been for these years, it has shown me a greater versatility of genius for every good word and work, than I had ever imagined. Indeed, if there were no special signs of genius in a man's career, character is able to become a capital substitute for it, in life's achievements and successes.

Many men, doubtless, have lived half a century in a city like this, and mingled in its commercial life, yet, I venture to say, that never did a man stamp a deeper local mark upon his generation, never was one more universally respected and beloved, as he came to his golden wedding with the business of his choice. He stands among us a representative man; yes, it may be truly said, in many respects, *the* representative man of Cleveland. So that there are thousands of people in this land to whom Mr. Handy is Cleveland, and Cleveland is Mr. Handy.

After all, gentlemen, we are only a small committee of his friends. If a rally should occur, of all the men, women and children in Cleveland, who share the feel-

ings of honor and affection with which you are greeting
him to-night, there would be no such limited company
as this, but a throng that would fill this broad avenue
from end to end, to represent the profound respect entertained for him by a constituency of wide and varied
extent.

Rarely has it become the privilege of any citizen to be
remembered by so many to whom he has been light in
the darkness—a staunch, generous helper in the time of
need. Such feelings as gather around him, are not
likely to be the mere blossoms of a spring, but the fade-
less evergreens of an eternity.

Under the many business pressures that tend to
weaken and degrade—in the face of social tendencies
and temptations that swerve so many; it is indeed a
noble manhood, gentlemen, that can face fifty years of
business scrutiny, of social and public criticism, and
gain the enviable record that your judgment and affection are giving him to-night.

These are days when sculpture is beginning to mem-
orize in our newer civilization those names that men
delight to honor. If ever a statue is erected in Cleveland, to represent business integrity, and commercial
wisdom, and righteous thrift, and wise benevolence, to
match the influence of patriotism that streams upon every
school boy as he looks up at Perry's monument on our
Public Square, it ought to be a statue of Truman P.
Handy.

But, sir, there is one element of our friend's character
and prosperity, one mighty influence of his life, to which,
perhaps, credit has not sufficiently been given for making
him what he is. In all justice, it demands eminent
mention.

I challenge you to look above the banking interest,
above the social congratulations, above the honorable
fame of civil standing, to the praise of God, and to the
name of our blessed Christianity, which is honored
through our guest, as it has honored him. He received
"the honor which cometh from God only," before he
could ever make the record that you are celebrating.

Should you ask him, I am sure he would tell you,
that underneath his energy, integrity, wisdom, generosity, through all these years, was the uplifting power of
a heavenly help—that his supreme ambition had been
to please his Divine Redeemer, to whom each day he
looked and humbly prayed, "Lead me only by Thy
light." His manliness has done much for him, but his
godliness has done more.

I ask only that he may be able to multiply his own
career—to perpetuate his influence—to have his own
perishable earthly life wrought into many an organization of imperishable power, and so ever live in Cleveland, mightily influencing our young men, and trans-
mitting to unborn generations, righteous examples that
shall never die.

Letters.

The Chairman:

The following letters have been received from absent friends whose presence would have contributed largely to the enjoyment of this occasion. The letters will speak for themselves.

From Gov. Charles Foster.

STATE OF OHIO,
EXECUTIVE DEPARTMENT,
OFFICE OF THE GOVERNOR.

COLUMBUS, O., May 15, 1882.

To the Directors of the Merchants' National Bank, Cleveland, Ohio.

GENTLEMEN: I am in receipt of your very kind invitation to join you in the complimentary dinner you propose to give Mr. Truman P. Handy, on the occasion of his fiftieth anniversary as a banker in Cleveland. I regret that engagements, that take me out of the State at the time named will prevent me from being present to enjoy the occasion with you.

I cannot forego this opportunity to express my great respect for the man you thus honor. It is indeed a rare occurrence, that fifty years of continuous business in one place and in one avocation is permitted to any man.

Mr. Handy has witnessed a marvelous change in the methods of conducting the business in which he has been engaged—from the old "Wild-cat" of the early days, through the prudent and safe business conducted by men of character and integrity under the charter of the "State Bank of Ohio," to the best of all systems of banking, the present national bank. He has enjoyed the sunshine, because he knew how to enjoy it; and has weathered the storm of fifty years, and stands to-day a conspicuous example of God's noblest work—an honest man.

I congratulate you that he is still with you, his faculties unimpaired, and unsullied in reputation; and if my wish could spare his life he would live to enjoy his friends at the centennial of his business life. I congratulate him on the fact that God has spared his life so long, and has permitted him to witness the wonderful growth of the beautiful city in which he lives, to enjoy the respect and confidence of all who know him, and that he has, by his many acts of kindness and generosity, both of his purse and his expression upon the conduct of his fellow mortals, endeared himself to his immediate friends and his countrymen in such a marked degree as to enable his friends to feel that he has "kept the faith," and his friends to feel that he is worthy of the crown that awaits him in the future.

Very truly yours,

CHARLES FOSTER.

From Mr. William G. Deshler.

COLUMBUS, O., May 15, 1882.

To the Directors of the Merchants' National Bank, Cleveland, Ohio,

DEAR SIRS: Please accept my thanks for your invitation to the complimentary dinner to Mr. T. P. Handy. Fearing that business engagements may prevent my presence, I write this note of acknowledgment with the understanding that, if possible, I will be with you in person; in that event this note shall be marked "paid." So long ago as 1842—a boy—teller of the old "Clinton Bank of Columbus," I wrote "pay to the order of T. P. Handy & Co." When I first saw Mr. Handy at Columbus the kindly interest he took in me, a boy, captured my respect and affection. During the intervening forty years the intercourse on my part, has been a constant growth of that feeling, and with hand clasping hand, I offer to my old friend my warmest congratulations, and ask that many years of usefulness may yet be his.

The business record of Mr. Handy is not confined to Cleveland.

Since the Bank Convention of 1837, at Columbus, down through the chain of old independent banks of 1842, the Ohio State banks, and the national bank system—through calm and storm, Mr. Handy has been suc-

cessful, active, and conspicuous, exerting an influence
for good that has been felt throughout our State.

Your beautiful and thriving city has, since 1837,
grown rapidly, proudly, and substantially, because of
your T. P. Handy; and now upon this, his "golden
semi-centennial," old age blesses him with the retrospect
of a life filled with useful service for the good of others,
as man, citizen, and banker.

Is it not the fulfillment of that divine promise to true
wisdom,—" In her right hand is length of days, and in
her left hand riches and honor?"

Very truly yours,

WILLIAM G. DESHLER.

From Rev. John W. Brown, S.T.D.

686 MAIN STREET.

BUFFALO, May 12, 1882.

MY DEAR MR. PERKINS: The occasion of meeting
my friend, Mr. Handy, to do honor to his long business
service, is a great attraction; but I am compelled to
forego the pleasure, as the early date, so soon after my
coming here, prevents. I wish you would give to Mr.
Handy, the remembrances of my warm personal regard,
and believe me to be, Sincerely yours,

JOHN W. BROWN.

From Mr. William A. Booth.

NEW YORK, May 13, 1882.

T. P. HANDY, ESQ.,

MY DEAR SIR: It was with much pleasure that I received the kind invitation to the complimentary dinner to be given on the 16th inst., and it informed me of the disposition of your friends in Cleveland to express their appreciation of your honorable course among them for the long period of fifty years. Such an expression in given worthily to but few men.

Your long and honorable course in the banking business—marked with enterprise, intelligence, integrity and success, entitles you to special consideration, and is a most worthy example to those who may succeed you.

The period of your active life has been one of the most eventful in the world's history. Its conflicts in business and banking relations have been many; to have survived them all, with reputation untarnished, may properly call forth the commendation of those associated with you in its active scenes.

I regret that I cannot be with you on an occasion so full of interest, and participate in its enjoyments.

With my best wishes, and the hope that your remaining days may be your best days,

I am, yours sincerely,

WILLIAM A. BOOTH.

Please express to your directors my regret that I cannot accept their kind invitation.

———

From Mr. John D. Rockefeller.

44 BROADWAY.

NEW YORK, May 13, 1882.

MY DEAR FRIEND: I regret exceedingly I cannot be present at the dinner, Tuesday evening, in honor of your fiftieth year as a banker in Cleveland. It would afford me great pleasure. I shall ever cherish very grateful recollections of your treatment of me as a young business man, and the very pleasant relations we have sustained for the last twenty-five years.

Hoping your life may be spared many years in the community which you have, by your noble example, so long benefitted and blessed,

I remain, with sincere regards,

Very truly yours,

JOHN D. ROCKEFELLER.

F. P. HANDY, Esq.,
Cleveland, Ohio.

From Mr. George S. Coe.

128 BROADWAY,

NEW YORK, May 13, 1882.

MY DEAR YOUNG FRIEND: I am greatly pleased and startled on the receipt of your kind invitation to meet you at dinner on Tuesday evening—pleased to know that your friends appreciate a real treasure when they have it, and startled that time has passed so rapidly over our youthful heads. Among all travelers in this fast age, none seems more rapid than he.

Fifty years in business life! and this is also true of me. A large portion of my experience has been made happier by having you as a friend and correspondent. May a kind Providence give you yet many more years of the same prosperity, usefulness, and vigor, that you have so eminently enjoyed in the past.

A review of these fifty years will doubtless form the subject of conversation at your social board. In 1830, when we entered business life, the tinder-box, flint and steel, with the tallow dip were modern utensils of domestic life, the axe, plow, shovel and hoe, the best implements of husbandry, and the Conestoga wagon the most rapid mode of land transportation. In that year the first locomotive engine was moved upon a track. That little event has made possible the reduction of this great continent to human habitation, and the increase of its population from twelve to fifty-two millions. All other forms of social intercourse and progress in the same ratio, have diminished the size of the earth for practical uses, and created an era so entirely new, that the contrast is bewildering. Life is now more crowded with cares, duties, and opportunities, if it is not with happiness, than when we began.

You have lived to see your good city grow up from a village, and may justly feel that it is a better place in every respect, because you have lived in it.

Greatly regretting that I cannot personally join your friends in congratulating you upon reaching so happily this important station upon life's journey, and with my best wishes for a long future.

I remain, my dear friend,

Very gratefully yours,

GEORGE S. COE.

TRUMAN P. HANDY, Esq.,
Cleveland, Ohio.

From Mr. Parker Handy.

MY DEAR BROTHER: I have just telegraphed you that "We have the Judge and wife visiting us, and that our Nellie is sick and I was obliged to decline your kind invitation with much regret." I had looked forward to this occasion with pleasure and fond anticipations of once more meeting many of my old Cleve-

land friends, and under peculiar circumstances, in paying
their kind regard to you in celebrating your semi-
centennial anniversary as a banker in Cleveland. What
great changes have taken place! The present generation cannot realize, but I will not expatiate on the differ-
ence between the present National banking system and
the various kinds of banks that we had years ago, including the "Red Ends" which exploded on the 1st of
May, 1845. In those days we had no money, and I
presume you will have with you, at your dinner, *several
friends* who could now command the means to have purchased the whole of the city, at that time, of both real
estate and all the personal property. No doubt you will
have a very enjoyable time, and my only regret is that
I cannot be with you. With many thanks for your kind
invitation, I remain,

Yours, very affectionately,

PARKER HANDY.

From Mr. James Rockwell.

UTICA, N. Y., May 18, 1882.

MY DEAR OLD FRIEND: The invitation to the banquet given you on the half century of your life in Cleveland has been received and invokes many memories of
the good days among the "30's," and that you had not
long been at your post when you so kindly invited me
to a position there with you.

Bankers to-day would look with astonishment at some of the statements of the old Commercial Bank of Lake Erie, showing a million and a quarter of circulation and no deposit of security—quite as much so at the *oppression* of those Southern Ohio bankers, who would save that circulation and demand redemption by draft on New York at forty-five to sixty days at par!

But you are largely entitled to the gratitude of the city, and citizens of Cleveland, for the many occasions you have exercised, in your official position, in fostering those interests which have increased the wealth of the town, and by the frequent help to young men just entering business life—my memory recurring to many loans where the security was on *character*, rather than *tangible* property—my personal knowledge being that the proceeds were used for board bills and expenses, which future earnings must be depended on to pay. What a change in the wealth of the city! And, while in '31 about every man, woman and child were known to me, now only the very old can be recognized in going through your beautiful streets; but if one tells me who his father or mother was, then I can locate his birthplace.

These old memories were not what I commenced to write, but rather to add my thanks (to the many you must have received on the occasion) for the personal kindness you so constantly and considerately gave to me in those days. So numerous indeed were they that

I would not attempt to enumerate; but it has seemed to
me very proper at this time to acknowledge and say
that, as years increase, all the obligations of those early
days are the more appreciated. So I rejoice to see all
those honors given you, and close by wishing you all
the good that age may bring to you.

Most truly,

JAMES ROCKWELL.

From Mr. Joseph Perkins.

CLEVELAND, O., May 15, 1882.

Directors of the Merchants' National Bank,

DEAR SIRS: Your kind invitation to attend the
semi-centennial of Mr. Handy's banking life is received.
It would afford me very unusual pleasure to participate
in the pleasures of that occasion, but my health compels
me most reluctantly to decline.

Most sincerely wishing Mr. Handy a long life to enjoy the honors of his long, honorable and beneficent life,
I am, with many thanks for your invitation,

Very truly yours,

JOSEPH PERKINS.

From Mr. Stevenson Burke.

CLEVELAND, O., May 15, 1882.

To E. R. Perkins, Esq., and Directors of the Merchants' National Bank.

GENTLEMEN: Until to-day I had expected to attend the banquet to be given your honored President Handy, to-morrow evening, but I am compelled to go to Chicago to-night, and hence will be absent at the time. Please accept my thanks for your kind invitation, and hopes that you will have a very enjoyable time.

Yours very truly,

STEVENSON BURKE.

From Mr. James M. Hoyt.

CLEVELAND, O., May 13, 1882.

E. R. Perkins, Esq., Merchants' National Bank.

SIR: Cordially appreciating the invitation of the Directors of the Merchants' National Bank, kindly sent to me, to be present at a complimentary dinner to be given to Truman P. Handy, on Tuesday evening next, I

greatly regret that my necessary absence from the city
at that time will prevent my attendance.

I should esteem it a pleasure and honor to express, by
my presence, did my engagements allow, my high regard for one who, for half a century, has been foremost
among our public benefactors.

Very truly yours,

JAMES M. HOYT.

From Mr. Charles A. Otis.

CLEVELAND, O., May 12, 1882.

To the Directors of the Merchants' National Bank.

GENTLEMEN: Thanking you for the kind invitation to attend a complimentary dinner to be given T. P.
Handy, Esq., on Tuesday evening next at the Union
Club, I regret that I am unable to be present, as I am
unexpectedly called from the city.

Yours, very truly,

CHARLES A. OTIS.

From Mr. Thurlow Weed.

NEW YORK, May 22, 1882.

MY DEAR OLD FRIEND: Many thanks for your kind and thoughtful letter which, with a Cleveland paper, was handed me by Mr. Gorham. Subsequently Mr. Van Schaick gave me a pleasant account of the interesting event which called him to Cleveland.

You, like myself, have much to be thankful for, for we have both been greatly favored. You received from your associates what your intelligence, enterprise, integrity and fidelity deserved, in the banquet tendered to you by the officers of the institution over which you preside, on the fiftieth anniversary of your connection with it. Few men reach, and none better deserve, such distinction. Having been affectionately remembered on the fiftieth anniversary of the establishment of the Albany *Evening Journal*, I can fully appreciate your feelings under circumstances even more auspicious.

You touch a tender chord in speaking of Thomas W. Olcott. I knew him intimately for more than sixty years; though, for forty years we were politically opposed, he was ever my warm, personal friend.

During the first six years after the *Evening Journal* was established, my name as maker or endorser for small sums went frequently into the Farmers' and Mechanics' Bank, and though, at that time, my "promises to pay" would not have been good in Wall street, Mr. Olcott discounted everything I asked for—a mark of confidence he never had occasion to regret.

I have known and felt much interest in all that concerned Ohio since she emerged from a Territorial to a State government. I knew General Morrison, Elisha Whittlesey, Mr. Vinton, Thomas Corwin, John W. Allen, Thomas Ewing and many other of her patriotic and distinguished sons. Chief Justice Carter, formerly a member of Congress from Ohio, when a boy was my apprentice.

I hope to have the pleasure of seeing you on your next visit to New York. Very truly,

THURLOW WEED.

www.ingramcontent.com/pod-product-compliance
Lightning Source LLC
Chambersburg PA
CBHW021527270326
41930CB00008B/1124